Laird

by Iain Gray

WRITING *to* REMEMBER

79 Main Street, Newtongrange,
Midlothian EH22 4NA
Tel: 0131 344 0414
E-mail: info@lang-syne.co.uk
www.langsyneshop.co.uk

Design by Dorothy Meikle
Printed by Blissetts
© Lang Syne Publishers Ltd 2024

All rights reserved. No part of this publication may be reproduced, stored or introduced into a retrieval system, or transmitted in any form or by any means (electronic, mechanical, photocopying, recording or otherwise) without the prior written permission of Lang Syne Publishers Ltd.

ISBN 978-1-85217-762-1

Laird

MOTTO:
Commit thy work to God
(Sinclair)

CREST:
A cockerel

TERRITORY:
Orkney, Caithness, Midlothian

NAME variations include:
 Lairde
 Leard
 Leird

Chapter one:

The origins of the clan system

by Rennie McOwan

The original Scottish clans of the Highlands and the great families of the Lowlands and Borders were gatherings of families, relatives, allies and neighbours for mutual protection against rivals or invaders.

Scotland experienced invasion from the Vikings, the Romans and English armies from the south. The Norman invasion of what is now England also had an influence on land-holding in Scotland. Some of these invaders stayed on and in time became 'Scottish'.

The word clan derives from the Gaelic language term 'clann', meaning children, and it was first used many centuries ago as communities were formed around tribal lands in glens and mountain fastnesses.

The format of clans changed over the centuries, but at its best the chief and his family held the land on behalf of all, like trustees, and the ordinary clansmen and women believed they had a blood relationship with the founder of their clan.

There were two way duties and obligations. An inadequate chief could be deposed and replaced by someone of greater ability.

Clan people had an immense pride in race. Their relationship with the chief was like adult children to a father and they had a real dignity.

The concept of clanship is very old and a more feudal notion of authority gradually crept in.

Pictland, for instance, was divided into seven principalities ruled by feudal leaders who were the strongest and most charismatic leaders of their particular groups.

By the sixth century the 'British' kingdoms of Strathclyde, Lothian and Celtic Dalriada (Argyll) had emerged and Scotland, as one nation, began to take shape in the time of King Kenneth MacAlpin.

Some chiefs claimed descent from ancient kings which may not have been accurate in every case.

By the twelfth and thirteenth centuries the clans and families were more strongly brought under the central control of Scottish monarchs.

Lands were awarded and administered more and more under royal favour, yet the power of the area clan chiefs was still very great.

The long wars to ensure Scotland's

independence against the expansionist ideas of English monarchs extended the influence of some clans and reduced the lands of others.

Those who supported Scotland's greatest king, Robert the Bruce, were awarded the territories of the families who had opposed his claim to the Scottish throne.

In the Scottish Borders country – the notorious Debatable Lands – the great families built up a ferocious reputation for providing warlike men accustomed to raiding into England and occasionally fighting one another.

Chiefs had the power to dispense justice and to confiscate lands and clan warfare produced a society where martial virtues – courage, hardiness, tenacity – were greatly admired.

Gradually the relationship between the clans and the Crown became strained as Scottish monarchs became more orientated to life in the Lowlands and, on occasion, towards England.

The Highland clans spoke a different language, Gaelic, whereas the language of Lowland Scotland and the court was Scots and in more modern times, English.

Highlanders dressed differently, had different

customs, and their wild mountain land sometimes seemed almost foreign to people living in the Lowlands.

It must be emphasised that Gaelic culture was very rich and story-telling, poetry, piping, the clarsach (harp) and other music all flourished and were greatly respected.

Highland culture was different from other parts of Scotland but it was not inferior or less sophisticated.

Central Government, whether in London or Edinburgh, sometimes saw the Gaelic clans as a challenge to their authority and some sent expeditions into the Highlands and west to crush the power of the Lords of the Isles.

Nevertheless, when the eighteenth century Jacobite Risings came along the cause of the Stuarts was mainly supported by Highland clans.

The word Jacobite comes from the Latin for James – Jacobus. The Jacobites wanted to restore the exiled Stuarts to the throne of Britain.

The monarchies of Scotland and England became one in 1603 when King James VI of Scotland (1st of England) gained the English throne after Queen Elizabeth died.

The Union of Parliaments of Scotland and England, the Treaty of Union, took place in 1707.

Some Highland clans, of course, and Lowland families opposed the Jacobites and supported the incoming Hanoverians.

After the Jacobite cause finally went down at Culloden in 1746 a kind of ethnic cleansing took place. The power of the chiefs was curtailed. Tartan and the pipes were banned in law.

Many emigrated, some because they wanted to, some because they were evicted by force. In addition, many Highlanders left for the cities of the south to seek work.

Many of the clan lands became home to sheep and deer shooting estates.

But the warlike traditions of the clans and the great Lowland and Border families lived on, with their descendants fighting bravely for freedom in two world wars.

Remember the men from whence you came, says the Gaelic proverb, and to that could be added the role of many heroic women.

The spirit of the clan, of having roots, whether Highland or Lowland, means much to thousands of people.

Meanwhile, many families proudly boast the heraldic device known as a Coat of Arms, as featured on our front cover.

The central motif of the Coat of Arms would originally have been what was sometimes borne on the shield of a warrior to distinguish himself from others on the battlefield.

Not featured on the Coat of Arms, but highlighted on page three, is the family motto and related crest – with the latter frequently different from the central motif.

Clan warfare produced a society where courage and tenacity were greatly admired

Chapter two:

Northern roots

A name that may appear to have 'lordly' connotations, 'Laird' in Scotland nevertheless originally denoted someone of a much lower social status.

Although 'laird' is the Old Scots pronunciation of the English 'lord', it is a term for the owner of an estate and was originally equivalent to 'esquire' in England and ranked above 'gentleman' but beneath 'baron'.

A 'bonnet laird', meanwhile, was a social rank below 'laird', but above those of 'husbandmen', or farmers – with 'bonnet' indicating that, in common with other non-landholders, this was the head gear customarily worn.

While some owners of estates in Scotland today may have pretensions to the designation of 'Laird', the Lord Lyon King of Arms of Scotland, the authority on such matters, is at pains to stress that the designation can only be held by those officially recognised by him through meeting the criteria that their estate is large and of long-standing.

Those who are officially recognised by the Lord Lyon are by tradition entitled to place 'The Much Honoured' before their name and to include the location of their 'lairdship'.

As an example, if a John Smith was officially recognised as having the lairdship of Newtongrange, he would be entitled to designate himself as 'The Much Honoured John Smith of Newtongrange'.

In recent years it has become common for very small plots of land to be sold on the market – with the buyers assuming that ownership of what may amount to only a few clumps of earth entitles them to assume a title.

Rather ludicrously, this has seen some buyers of these 'souvenir' plots of land proudly assuming an heraldic Coat of Arms, complete with motto and crest and dubbing themselves 'lord', 'lady' or 'baron.'

As a surname, 'Laird' first appears in the Scottish historical record – in the now redundant form 'Lawrid' – in 1257 when a Roger Lawrid of Berwick, in the Borders, was involved in a land transaction with the abbot of Kelso Abbey.

In the redundant form of 'Loerd', Thomas de Loerd was a signatory to a humiliating treaty of fealty to England's conquering King Edward I, known as the Hammer of the Scots.

Signed at Berwick by 1,500 Scottish earls, bishops and burgesses, the parchment was known as the *Ragman Roll* because of the profusion of ribbons that dangled from the seals of the signatories.

Just over 250 years later, in the more familiar spelling variant 'Lairde', a Thomas Lairde is recorded as a witness in Glasgow relating to a legal matter, while in the even more familiar form 'Laird', a David Laird is recorded in 1574 as a Church minister in Foveran, Kirkwall, in Orkney.

Sources have found the Laird name also appears from early times in Orkney and Caithness as 'Leard' and 'Leird', and this link with the far northeast of Scotland is intriguing – because the Lairds are regarded as a sept, or sub-branch, of the two powerful clans Clan Keith and Clan Sinclair.

Clan Keith, who held Lowland territory in East Lothian in addition to Caithness and Aberdeenshire, have the motto 'Truth prevails' and crest of a stag's head, while Clan Sinclair also held Lowland territory, in Midlothian, in addition to Orkney and Caithness.

Derived from the Gaelic *clanna*, meaning

'children', a clan was a close-knit tribal grouping settled in a particular territory and whose members – or 'children', or 'kin' – owed unswerving loyalty to a chief who, in turn, was bound by duty and honour to protect them.

Not all members of a clan, such as the Lairds, necessarily shared the same surname as the chief – known as *ceann-cinnidh*, meaning 'head and chief of the family' – and these 'kindred of the clan', or 'kinsfolk', were recognised, as they are to this day, as septs, or sub-branches of the clan.

As such, they are entitled to share in the clan's heritage and traditions that include the right to display its tartan and heraldry of crest and motto – in the case of Clan Sinclair the motto 'Commit thy work to God' and crest a cockerel.

Despite their kinship with Clan Keith, it is with the Sinclairs, along with others including the Clynes, Linklaters, Lyalls and Masons that the Lairds appear to have the closest bond – explained largely in part by what may well have been a shared and distant origin in Norway.

Research into the early roots of the Lairds and Sinclairs has identified old farm names in the western reaches of Norway beginning with the suffix 'Leir' – for example 'Leirdal', indicating a landowner.

It is reasonable to speculate that those designated 'Leir' were among those who later adopted the Sinclair name – or retained the name that later became known as 'Leard', 'Leird' or 'Laird' in Orkney and Caithness.

It is also reasonable to speculate they were also among those Norse raiders who embarked in longships from their Norwegian homeland to raid, ravage and pillage before settling in what became known as 'Norse-man's-land' – better known today as Normandy, in France.

By 912 these raiders had risen to great power and influence, owning vast tracts of land and mighty strongholds. A force to be reckoned with, their leader, Rollo, signed a treaty with Charles III of France that created him Count of Rouen.

The treaty was signed at the castle of St Clair-sur-Epte, and it was through this location that the name 'St Clair' arose, more popularly recognised today as Sinclair, and reckoned to be one of the oldest surnames in Europe.

Nine Sinclair knights fought with great distinction on the side of their fellow Norman, William the Conqueror, at the Battle of Hastings in 1066, a battle that paved the way for Norman supremacy in England, and it was either one of these knights, or a relative, who later settled in Scotland.

A Henry Sinclair is recorded as holding lands in Lothian in 1162, while Sir William Sinclair, a guardian of the young Alexander III, was granted the barony of Rosslyn, in Midlothian, in 1280.

Another Sinclair, Sir Henry Sinclair, fought with his kinsfolk such as the Lairds in the cause of Scotland's freedom at the Battle of Bannockburn in 1314, and was also one of the signatories of the famous Declaration of Arbroath of 1320, while his brother William, Bishop of Dunkeld, led an army that repulsed a force of English at Donibristle in 1317.

Two of Sir Henry's sons, Sir William and Sir John Sinclair, were among the knights who had been entrusted by Robert the Bruce on his death bed to place his heart before the Holy Sepulchre in Jerusalem.

They left Scottish shores along with others faithful to his wishes, including Sir James Douglas, but a European crusade to the Holy Land never materialised, and the band instead sailed for Spain where King Alfonso XI of Castile was set to mount a campaign against the Moorish kingdom of Granada.

The battle-hardened Scots were gratefully welcomed and, in August of 1330 formed part of Alfonso's Christian army that was besieging the castle of Teba.

In a vicious battle against the foe, Sir James and his compatriots were surrounded and most of them killed – including Sir James and the Sinclair brothers – but not before Douglas had hurled the precious casket before him, shouting: "Lead on brave heart, I'll follow thee" or, as other accounts state: "Go first as thou hast always done."

The casket was recovered from the carnage of the battlefield by Sir Symon Locard and the few Scots who had survived and returned to Scotland – where it was buried in Melrose Abbey.

A grandson of Sir Henry Sinclair, meanwhile, is recognised as having laid the foundation for the Sinclairs' great territories in the distant northern realms of Scotland – where the Laird name is found in a number of variants – through his marriage to Isabella, Countess of Orkney, while one of his descendants, also named Henry, inherited the title of Earl of Orkney in 1379.

Known as the Prince of Orkney, the blood of his seafaring Norse ancestors coursed strongly through his veins.

He conquered the Faroe Islands in 1391, gained control of Shetland, and in 1398 embarked on a remarkable voyage across the Atlantic in a fleet of twelve ships, along with the Venetian navigator Antonio Zeno.

A rare chart known as the Zeno Map, in addition to archaeological finds, reveals that they explored modern day Labrador, Nova Scotia, and Massachusetts, indicating that a Sinclair may well have been responsible for discovering America a century before Columbus.

The northern power of the Sinclairs was increased in 1455 when King James II granted William, the third Sinclair Earl of Orkney, the earldom of Caithness –while the Earl of Caithness is recognised to this day as chief of the Clan Sinclair.

Chapter three:

Master builders

Standing on the edge of the scenic Esk Valley near the village of Roslin, in Midlothian, and attracting thousands of visitors every year is the mysterious Rosslyn Chapel, built in 1446 by William Sinclair, who was created Lord Sinclair in 1449.

Founded as a collegiate church and consecrated to St Matthew it is thought to encode in stone a mystery that links a band of warrior monks who were known as the Knights Templar, the origins of Scottish Freemasonry, and a secret relating to the Holy Grail – a theme of the best-selling 2003 Dan Brown novel *The Da Vinci Code* and the 2006 film of the name.

It had been intended that the chapel be built in the form of a cross, with a tower in the centre but it was never completed; only the east transept and the choir were built.

Finished in a style described as 'florid Gothic', it is famous for its Apprentice's Pillar, which stands in the south east corner.

Decorated with four wreaths of flowers,

spiralling from base to crown, it is the subject of a curious legend that the Master Mason, jealous of the skill of a young apprentice who sculpted the pillar, killed him with a blow to the forehead.

With strange echoes of Freemasonic legend, three stone heads at the west of the chapel commemorate this slaying.

One is thought to be the apprentice's mother, and is known as The Widowed Mother, while one depicts the apprentice with a gash above his right eye, and the other depicts the Master Mason.

This is taken as evidence that the stone masons who built the chapel were privy to esoteric knowledge.

This had been entrusted to them originally through Knights Templar who had been granted refuge in Scotland – despite being outlawed by Papal Bull throughout the rest of Europe in 1307 on a series of trumped-up charges including rejection of accepted Church doctrine on Christ.

The Templars, who had been established by Papal sanction in 1118 to guard the pilgrim routes to the Holy Land, are thought to have excavated the ruins of Solomon's Temple in Jerusalem, and unearthed an awesome secret relating to Christianity.

Some claim the secret may have been in the form of ancient parchments – or even the famed Holy Grail of the Last Supper itself. Another theory is that the grail may not be an actual vessel, or cup, but a secret relating to the bloodline of Christ.

A persistent claim is that a body of refugee Templars fought on the side of Robert the Bruce at Bannockburn, and that their secret knowledge was later transmitted, through what became Scottish Freemasonry, to some of Scotland's noblest families, including the Sinclairs.

Sir William Sinclair, some believe, may actually have built Rosslyn Chapel as a repository for the secrets of the Templars.

Twelve Sinclair barons are known to be buried in sealed vaults beneath the chapel, laid to rest in full armour – and who knows what else may lie gathering the dust of centuries in these vaults.

From construction in stone to construction in iron, William and John Laird were the enterprising Scottish father and son who founded what became the Cammell shipyard, building vessels that ply the seven seas under the name to this day.

Born in 1780 in Greenock, near Glasgow, William Laird was aged 30 when he moved to

Liverpool initially to help in the development of his family's rope-making business but, two years later, set up a steamship company to exploit the opportunities offered by trade between Liverpool and Glasgow.

Although this proved successful, Laird was ambitious for more success and, in 1824 and in partnership with others, bought land adjoining what was then the small village of Birkenhead, opposite Liverpool on an inlet of the River Mersey, on the Wirral.

Later also setting up the Birkenhead Iron Works with another partner, when this failed he set up in businesses with his elder son John.

Born in Greenock in 1805, John Laird had been working as a solicitor's clerk when he joined his father in the boiler-making business William Laird and Son.

What was to revolutionise their business and fortunes came in 1828 when they received an order to construct iron ships for use on canals and lakes in Ireland.

Realising that the techniques employed in making ships – bending iron plates and riveting them together – were similar to those used in manufacturing boilers, they produced their first vessel, a pre-fabricated iron lighter, in 1829.

Further orders followed, including pre-fabricated river steamers including, in 1834, the paddle steamer *John Randolph*, for use in Savannah, Georgia, and America's first iron vessel.

A screw-propelled steamer, *Robert F. Stockton*, followed five years later while, during the American Civil War of 1861 to 1865, they flouted Britain's policy on trade by building vessels for the Confederacy including the raider CSS *Alabama*.

In the meantime, William Laird had commissioned the Scottish architect James Gillespie Graham to design a new town close to his shipyard – and this became the centre of what had been the village of Birkenhead.

He died in 1841 and his son John was joined in partnership in the business by his three sons.

John Laird retired in 1861, leaving the running of the business to his sons, while he entered politics and served as MP (Member of Parliament) for Birkenhead from 1861 to 1874.

Responsible along with his father for the development of the town and a noted benefactor, he established a school, hospital and the Laird School of Art.

He died in 1874 while the company, now

Laird Brothers, merged in 1903 with Johnson Cammell and Company, of Sheffield, to form Cammell Laird.

In addition to building passenger trains for use in India, rolling stock for the London Underground and armoured road trains – forerunners of the tank – for use in the Boer War, ships they designed and built include HMS *Ark Royal* in 1937, the passenger liner *Mauretania*, launched in 1938 and, in 1941, the battleship HMS *Prince of Wales*.

Along with the rest of the shipbuilding industry, Cammell Laird was nationalised in 1977 as British Shipbuilders and subsequently went through a bewildering number of changes of ownership.

Returning to the private sector in 1986 as part of Vickers Shipbuilding and Engineering (VSEL), of Barrow-in-Furness, it constructed nuclear submarines including HMS *Unicorn*.

But the shipyard closed in 1993 and part of it was leased as a ship repair facility to Coastline Group, which later bought part of the yard and adopted the Cammell Laird name.

In 2007, the right to the name was acquired by Northwestern Shiprepairers and Shipbuilders and it has since enjoyed a healthy order book.

These include, in 2010, an order to supply the flight decks for the state-of-the-art aircraft carrier HMS *Queen Elizabeth*.

William and John Laird, founders of the famous business, would meanwhile have doubtlessly been bemused to learn what had been the proposed name for a Royal Research Ship built by the company for the British Antarctic Survey.

Entering service in 2019, the public had been invited to propose a name and the most popular choice was *Boaty McBoatface*.

More sober minds prevailed, however, and it was named RRS *Sir David Attenborough*, in honour of the naturalist and environmental campaigner of the name – although *Boaty McBoatface* was conceded as the name for one of the vessel's underwater vehicles.

Chapter four:

On the world stage

In the highly competitive world of sport, Martin Laird is the champion Scottish golfer, born in Glasgow in 1982, who plays on the PGA (Professional Golfers Association) Tour.

Playing junior golf at Kirkintilloch Golf Club and at youth level at Hilton Park Golf Club, he was aged 17 when, with the assistance of College Prospects of America, he took up a golf scholarship at Colorado State University.

Having learned to play left-handed but then switching to right, he played for the Colorado State Rams and, turning professional after leaving college, won the 2004 Denver Open.

He progressed steadily, earning his PGA Tour card for 2008 and securing a place at the Open Championship the following year, but missing the cut by only two strokes.

Only a week before, he had finished tenth in the Scottish Open while later in the year he enjoyed his first PGA Tour win at the Justin Timberlake Shriners Hospital for Sick Children Open.

This made him the first Scot, since Sandy Lyle in 1988, to win a PGA Tour event in the United States, and he became the highest ranked Scot, at No. 108, in the Official World Golf Rankings. His biggest win to date came in 2011 at the Arnold Palmer Invitational – earning just over $1m dollars.

On the ice, **Anne Laird** is the Scottish curler who, in 2002, was part of the team that won the gold medal at the World Curling Championship, in the role of lead. Born in Musselburgh in 1970, she also won a bronze medal for her country playing, again as lead, in the 1991 World Junior Championships.

On the cricket pitch, **Bruce Laird**, born in 1950 in Mount Lawley, Western Australia, is the former opening batsman who played 13 'Supertests' in World Series Cricket and 21 Tests.

From cricket to baseball, **Gerald Lee Laird III** is the American former catcher who played in Major League Baseball (MLB) for teams including the St Louis Cardinals, Detroit Tigers and Arizona Diamondbacks.

From sport to film, **Jack Laird** was the award-winning American screenwriter, director, producer and actor whose big screen role as an actor was in the 1934 *The Circus Clown*.

Born in Los Angeles in 1923, he moved from acting to a role behind the camera, winning Primetime Emmy Award nominations for his work on *Night Gallery*, *Kojak* and *Ben Casey*.

Impressed by the acting abilities of Leslie Nielsen, he made a number of 'made for television' films starring the actor – the first in that genre – including, from 1964, *See How They Run*.

Also inspired by the novels of the American horror writer H.P. Lovecraft, he based a number of his *Night Gallery* television shows on his work, including the spine-tingling *Professor Peabody's Last Lecture*; he died in 1991.

In the world of literature, **Elizabeth Laird** is the award-winning children's author and travel writer born in New Zealand in 1943 to a Scottish father and New Zealander mother. As a traveller to such far-flung places such as Ethiopia, she has collected and published a number of folk tales, while her 2003 *The Garbage King* was the winner of the Scottish Arts Council Children's Book of the Year.

Shortlisted five times for the Carnegie Medal for British Children's Literature and a judge since 2010 for the Walter Scott Prize for Historical Fiction, her other best-selling works include the 1988 *Red Sky in the Morning*, the 2001 *Jake's Tower* and, from 2007, *Crusade*.

Born in 1975 in Cookston, Co. Tyrone, **Nicholas Laird** is the Northern Irish poet and novelist who married best-selling British novelist Zadie Smith in 2004, after the couple met while students at Cambridge University.

His first collection of poems, *To a Fault*, published in 2005, was nominated for the Forward Prize for Best First Collection, while his collection On Purpose was winner of the 2008 Somerset Maugham Award and the Geoffey Faber Memorial Prize.

A master of words whose legacy survives to this day, **Charlton Laird** was the American lexicographer, linguist, essayist and novelist responsible for the 1971 edition of *Webster's New World Thesaurus* of words and phrases.

Born in 1901 in Nashau, Iowa and Distinguished Professor of Humanities from 1945 to 1968 at the University of Nevada, Reno, and utilising his knowledge to explain the English language to the layperson, his 1971 edition of the thesaurus, revised a number of times since, remains a standard work.

An inductee of the Nevada Writers Hall of Fame, he died in 1984.

Bearers of the Laird name have also excelled in the complex world of the sciences.

The first woman to be accepted to conduct research at Cambridge University's famed Cavendish Laboratory, **Elizabeth Laird** was the Canadian physicist born in 1874 in Owen Sound, Ontario.

Graduating from the London Collegiate Institute in 1893 and then studying at Toronto University and later earning a doctorate in physics and mathematics from Bryn Mawr College, Pennsylvania, she was nevertheless denied an exhibition scholarship, which would have allowed her to carry out experimental research abroad, because of her gender.

But the Nobel Prize-winning physicist Sir J.J. Thomson, Cavendish Professor of Physics at Cambridge University, proved more open-minded and allowed her to work in his laboratory – the first woman to do so.

Chair for nearly forty years of the physics department of Mount Holyoke College, in South Hadley, Massachusetts, she died in 1969, while Asteroid (16192) *Laird* is named in her honour.

In contemporary times and in the realm of workers' rights, **Gavin Laird**, born in Clydebank in 1933, was the Scottish trade union official who served as general secretary of the Amalgamated Engineering and Electrical Union (AEEU); honoured with a knighthood in 1995, he died in 2017.

One particularly daring and enterprising bearer of the Laird name was the pioneering American pilot, aircraft builder and businessman Emil Matthew Laird, more popularly known as **Matty Laird**, born in 1896 and raised in Chicago.

His first job was office boy in a bank – but his abiding passion was flight and, when aged only 15, he built a rudimentary aircraft from a bicycle with glider wings attached. A monoplane followed shortly afterwards which, in 1913, he managed to lift 10ft (3.0m) off the ground.

Achieving much greater heights, he learned to fly and built with the help of friends the Laird Baby Biplane – flying it as a dare-devil 'barnstorming' pilot throughout the Midwest.

The Laird 1915 Biplane then followed, in which he performed death-defying aerobatic stunts such as the loop-the-loop while, in 1917, he nearly lost a leg and broke a number of bones while test flying another designer's aircraft that crashed after entering a spin from which he could not recover.

Founding the E.M. Laird Airplane Company

in Chicago in 1923, he went on to build a number of commercial aircraft racing models including the Laird LC-DW500 Super Solution biplane.

It was this aircraft, piloted by Major James H. Doolittle – later to claim fame as commander during the Second World War of the 'Doolittle Raid' over some of the main Japanese islands in April of 1942 – that was the first winner, in 1931, of the Bendix Trophy Race from Burbank, California to Cleveland.

An inductee of the Kansas Aviation Hall of Fame, the aircraft pioneer died in 1982.

From feats of aviation to the world of music, **Luke Laird**, born in 1978 in Harstown, Pennsylvania, is the American country music songwriter and producer who has written and co-written more than twenty U.S. Billboard Country Music chart No. 1 hits that include Kenny Chesney's 2014 *American Kids*.

In a much different music genre, **Richard Laird**, born in Dublin in 1941, is the Irish bassist and former house bassist at Ronnie Scott's Jazz Club, London, who also played with John McLaughlin's Mahavishnu Orchestra.

On the dance floor, **Walter Laird**, born in 1920, was the British dance champion and coach credited with having been a major influence in the development of Latin American dancing in Britain.

Switching from traditional ballroom to Latin American dancing at the end of the Second World War and, along with his partner Lorraine Reynolds, World Professional Latin Dance Champion in 1962, 1963 and 1964 and author of *Technique of Latin Dancing*, he died in 2002.

Expressing his creative talent through comic book art and writing, **Peter Laird** is the co-creator of the highly successful *Teenage Mutant Ninja Turtles* series of comics.

Born in 1954 in Dover, New Hampshire, it was after teaming up with fellow writer and illustrator Kevin Eastman and thanks to a loan from Eastman's uncle, that in 1984 the pair produced their first issue of *Teenage Mutant Ninja Turtles* – that has since spawned lucrative film and merchandising spin-offs.

Speaking of his early days, Laird recalls how the second issue of the comic netted them a profit of $2000 each.

This allowed them, he says, "to write and draw full-time: it was enough to pay the rent, pay the bills, and buy enough macaroni and cheese and pencils to live on."